TRIDENTS OF GLASS
AND OTHER POEMS

David M. Antonelli

The cover page shows an image taken by NASA Voyager in 1989.

Neptune is the remotest planet in the solar system, but also has its most violent and unpredictable storms.

Tridents of Glass

I

I watch my days
searching
for the transcendental

a moment in time
or better
a wing of a bird
somewhere on that dark wall
fluttering

a kind of dance
speaking to my yearning
but always
an island
unable to reach me

II

Where was that dark chord
first struck?
On some broken bell
submerged
out there,
forever concealed
from human vision?

And when I last kissed
you, was your hair
not blonde enough
or my eyes too blue?

This was the night
I knew it would be,
a place of torpedoes
and lozenges,
where the sick
collect their thermometers
speaking of rebellion,

A hovering black chalice
hammered out
from some bland humidity,
which taunts me
to this day.

Yet still I would take
your lips,

a door to regret,
wet without velvet
or caprice,
on that journey
to forever –
whatever that means.

III

Startled by the cable cars
I turned to see two children
Playing in the street -
Lightning in their hair,

As though the soil was no longer
Pleasurable, or the rain
Suddenly too perilous
To risk a pathway to the stars.

Speak to me, speak to me:
Tell me who you are
And what dreams still devour
The cradle of your nights,

So nothing can reclaim you
And drag you back into
That yet deeper cradle
From which you once emerged.

There, on the *Unter den Linden*,
It seemed we all converged
On that silence, where
Night was swallowed once again

By more impatient minds,
And we spun like rings
Around a fabulous Saturn
Of our own creation.

And when the children
Finally noticed me watching,
They recoiled - or was it just a laugh? –
and disappeared into a crowd.

IV

You, who always wore felt, lecturing
without remorse
On the murders of Odysseus.

You, who paraded, naked and indignant,
through Rose Bowl boulevards
Of snow and glass.

You, who ride on the back of the scorpion,
forever craving
Its fatal poison.

You, who burned with pious eyes all
evidence of your crimes,
Searching for what you call redemption.

You, who wail like the sun, when only the
moon
Is singing in the sky.

You, who were handcuffed without
subpoena for worshipping Venus
On the turnpikes of Fort Lauderdale.

You, who languish in your Palace of Death,
demanding interrogation
And torture as your final reprieve.

You, who host high dignitaries at insidious
feasts, laughing from inside
Your hall of magnets.

You, who hide beneath the shadow of an
orange tree, yearning
For the end of time.

You, who wander through your valleys of
genocide, the scent of virtue
Still lingering in the air.

You, who danced with hollow glee as you
whispered our first travesty in my ear:
Saint of the night.

Guide me through your corridors of burning
rain, my mouth
Forever open to the anguish of the sky.

V

You looked so tempting
there: a statue in the garden,
starlight curled
beneath your brow,
a look of expectancy
projected on your face
as though you had always
been waiting
to rise above me –
a bed of helium
scattered to the clouds.

With the image of Normandy
now trembling on your skin
but without bullets or parachutes,
we made a gift
of that silence
to whatever muse
we were never quite certain
was standing
there beside us.

But life is always like this
in retrospect,
you said
and will always say –
I am sure,
as I am sure
of no other thing

in this world.

VI

Do you remember
that afternoon
at the Jackson Pollock
retrospective
when you whispered
in my ear
"If Kim Jong-un
had fronted
the Sex Pistols
or Lucretius
was the Beatles'
first drummer,
it all would have been
the same anyway"?

But autumn passed
so quickly that year,
the golden leaves
gathering in scented
cesspools, our children
giggling in sheds
with skeletons
of rusted plumbing,
almost festive
in their pumpkin-coloured finery,
as we slid together
down the throat
of yet another cold winter.

And I only realized
The day you left
for good
that it was exactly
what we thought
it would be,
with every instant
having the chance
to be utterly different
if we had only
spent less time
watching the snow
gathering
on the windows
of our old Chevrolet
forever waiting
for some vernal breath
to tip its hat
to the coming Spring.

VII

With the breath of the Titans
I shall grind my jewelled
Daggers, blessing

Your naked breasts
On the beds of eternity
Where once we strayed

From more desolate plains
To the birthplace
Of Angels and Sin

Balanced on your lips
Of satin and fire
A tightrope walker

Losing his way above
The abyss, trembling
Lest he dare look up

Or down on the open bed
Before him, where *everything*
is fear and chance at last.

VIII

Cities, where Senators debate the
pronunciation of lost diphthongs, if only
To trade in human organs.

Cities, where glamorous models play
fictitious mandolins at the gates
Of demolished casinos.

Cities, where the shadow of a vanquished
God blesses
The headboard of the Idiot Child.

Cities, where the kiss of the cobra is less
treacherous
Than the bite of the marigold.

Cities, where convicted Cardinals transact in
currencies of dark matter
And plutonium.

Cities, where diamonds are sold for the price
of wind, and plagues
Assume the form of some new Calculus.

Cities, where mirrors are fashioned from
lies, and perfume is extracted
From the mouths of gargoyles.

Cities, where children play behind the
rainbow doors of mausoleums,
A telescope their only weapon.

Cities, where career Adonises abandon their
regimens of sex and lithium
In search of a jar of marbles.

Cities, where great dignitaries expound on
foreign invasion, while choirs
Sing circus songs of benediction.

Cities, where legions of patent leather
briefcases explode in showers
Of violets and polygamy.

Banish me from your silicone palaces, if
only to adorn me with trophies
Of hurricanes and electronic money.

IX

I wrote an equation
once,
to predict the smell
of Jasmine
on your skin.
But soon the world opened –
not a pistil
naked in the Sun,
but something more
weightless and terrifying,
already toothed
by the diamonds
of the night.

And if we could just stand
there, *invisible* –
consumed by that dark turbine
where nothing speaks
but those things we once imagined,
what would become
of us, then?
(as though this question
ever really mattered)

Could we ration
our breath, devouring
our very essence
in exchange for a stake
in that random territory

now lost between us:
the lines of a poem
not yet written,
but forever hovering
mere centimetres
from the poet's eye?

Voices that speak to us,
Voices that listen to us,
Voices we are not
so certain ever existed,

Tell us now that *this*
is what we will become
and always be.

X

With what new grace
could I knock on your door –
your final smile
still crackling there
in the darkness,
only slightly failing
to delay the arrival
of the coming Ice Age?

If only we could return
to those perilous
mountains
that once rejoiced for us,
would the wilderness
still threaten to engulf us,
as it did that night
we left our new-born
beneath the Northern Lights
(a white owl hunched
there in the evergreens)
to suckle with the wolves?

Would I become
some new D'Artagnan,
or just an Instagram image
of that person you once
met for coffee
that day in the chalet,
the sound of unseen branches

rustling in our ears?

The question
is neither light nor dark,
you say. It simply is,
born as always
from the hollering
beneath the cradle.

Praise be to light
and memories
of your satin skin,
drank to drunkenness
every night,
when even the sound
of shower stalls
hissed through
adjacent walls,
our bed adorned
with stains
of radon and blood.

Since you left,
these days have amassed
great weight,
towering somewhere
in the fractured sky,
a Colossus of Rhodes
lost in the deltas of the night:
past here, present
there, a lost ray

reflecting off
some other star.

XI

Your eyes surprised me:
screaming like a child
from inside a lunar trench,
when every newsroom said

you had nothing left to say.
Oh, ballerina with your lips
of starlight and fire, arm me
with your last pirouette,

so I can wander weightless
in your pale gravity until
the Sun implodes. "If only
life was really like this,"

you replied, laughing, "We
have so much left to do today
and the dusk is already gathering
outside the window."

Of course, I stood there thinking,
there will always be unbought
groceries and those theatre tickets
received as gifts but never used.

Because in every sensation
lies a certain numbness,
and from every dictate gushes
new fountains of uncertainty.

Your eyes returned – star anise
lifting me from my seat.
It was the year of some pandemic
I have long since forgotten

and Drake was playing on the radio.
It was then that I wondered
how it was that you could get
through life, breathing every day,

yet dying with every turn
of that lunar path.
The dusk has evaporated
and now I see what we thought

was its broken grey light,
and all the dull exigencies
that go with it, was really just
frost on the window.

XII

Those who study the plight of the octopus,
reeking
Of tobacco and infinity.

Those who lock refugees in meat trucks,
only to be scalped and traded
In markets for baskets of lemurs.

Those who fornicate with tongues of
notaries, paralyzed
In their beds of arsenic and obsidian.

Those who paint their hatred with golden
sables, scraping crusted enamels
From the canvases of Genesis.

Those who scream into the funnel of night,
screaming yet again
In the bitter light of dawn.

Those who rejoice in the birth of the
Succubus, plagiarising Italian operas
In the sanctuary of their attics.

Those who rescue nameless victims from
crumbling hospitals,
Their pockets filled with stolen sutures.

Those who fraternise with the gleaming
Centurions of climate change,
Forever imbibing from the horn of the
narwhale.

Those who drink the milkshake of
forgetfulness, still longing
For the entropy of night.

Those who stage secret festivals in the
mouths of dormant volcanos,
Celebrating the dawn of the Kali Yuga.

Those who play obscure harmonies on the
rims of their sunglasses, entertaining
Only the occasional Leprechaun or lost
buffalo.

Praise be the anthems of your wandering
Kings - those uncontrollable Masters
who once rose so quietly from the abyss.

XIII

"There's a Starman waiting in the sky,
but he decided not to meet us
and sold the World instead,"
I heard a young girl singing
on her skateboard
some bright Spring day.
Or did I get the story wrong,
like I always do,
mixing my own failings
with someone else's fancy?

But that was only half the story
as Winter brought us light that year,
putting one man's Kandor
inside another man's Bell Jar.
With Superman amongst us
we always felt protected.
We had no reason not to.

For with every act of thinking is the Word.
And in every last presumption is the Word.
But that Word is not God, but something
else
we always carry inside us, but never can
define.

We rode down the slopes
lined with clumps of evergreen,

our wooden sleds
broken, but their runners
still cutting through the snow.
And when we were done
I thought I wanted to kiss
that red-haired girl by the fire
until her boyfriend walked in
and she seemed happy
to just let him claim her, as if
with a ticket at a coat check.
But that never stopped me
From dreaming.

Living was easy with eyes closed
misunderstanding all we saw.
And I am sure we will keep it that way.
We have no reason not to.

XIV

If Orpheus had driven a tank
would he have thrown
that last worried gaze
at Eurydice as he rolled
so inexorably
away from the Underworld,
retrieving her at last?
Or would he have spared her
that immortality,
boosted by his armour
and no longer fearing death –
finding its scent of darkness
a deeper perfume
than any eternal silence?

And if I were to become
some new Barbarian,
drinking fermented blood
from a brief case of snakeskin
and bone,
(yet somehow still weakened
before your greater light)
would you turn me
from your door,
stranger that I am,
or could we wander
together as two children –
eye to eye,
forever reckless and forgiving

beneath the wilderness
of the Sun?

As I whispered these questions
into your ear,
I suddenly saw them for what they were:
clumsy metaphors, aimed
at nothing
that really mattered
or ever would –
projections of my mind,
born from nothing
but tangles of ruthless neurons
wailing through the night.

With the universe
now balanced on a blade
I watched you sleeping –
no doubt lost in dreams
of some bright Champagne summer
(or so I guessed)
filled with lilacs and tall sycamores,
and you hardly even stirred.

XV

Even the lilies shattered
as you pulled off your blouse,
My Bloody Valentine

droning from the other room,
while someone shot hoops
in front of the garage next door

the sound of the basketball
syncopated by some wild irony
with the rhythm of our sex.

But that was never enough,
The muses of our flesh
forever building that wall

between us. And even if those
mountains could somehow allow us
to scale their bleeding slopes at last,

becoming more pastoral, a place for Chagall
and his rainstorms of violins and goats,
I could never fully bask in your

ultraviolet gaze. So I created your
doppelganger, hoping to possess
you and escape you all at once,

only to realise it was still you –

only it wasn't, stained now
by the fingers of my creation,

distorted beyond all recognition,
a living Facebook ad in bold text reading
"Each man kills the things he loves."

XVI

Roads, once so bare and open, now left
cratered and lonely
By the lab rats of logic and Versace.

Roads, once speaking to us in calming
cypher from verandas of polished steel,
Now only screaming the terror of our
creation.

Roads, once forging sonatas on vast tarmac
pianos, now entertaining
The Duchesses of lies and endless orgasm.

Roads, once traversed by bankers and
clairvoyants, long since discarding
Their guidebooks for invisible palaces in the
sky.

Roads, once chanting violent slogans of war,
now passing them off
As telepathic messages from some great new
tomorrow.

Roads, once leading us to clear and
sparkling oceans, where children
Now only gape into the mouths of neutron
stars.

Roads, once following the gentle contours of
your skin, now etched by rivers
Of blood and endless tears.

Roads, once mistaken for conduits to
uncharted lands, now only leading us
To cities we never left in the first place.

Roads, once enlisting bland Homeric spies
to enforce false dictates,
Now just Rubicon threats of incarceration.

Roads, once guarded by tiny lizards and
desert birds, now inadmissible
To anyone who dares attempt passage.

Roads, once execrated in blasphemous
incantations, now posing
As the last bastion of piety and reason.

Lead us through your mires and electric
fields to a Paradise
Of helicopters and ecstasy.

XVII

If I could scale the Eifel Tower
(full knowing my fear of heights)
and play the passing clouds,
tuning their icy vapours
as though strings
of a great guitar,
would that be my final
victory, or would it end
in embarrassment,
transforming our love
into some Fox News spectacle –
The WWF, with me against
The Rock at last?

"True love never ends,"
you said, eyes suddenly
narrowed to a pair
of laser scalpels
hovering in the darkness,
the window already
leaking the first
light of dawn.

But when you continued
with a simple yawn
I saw at last,
as though scrawled across
your coffee-stained
map of the constellations,

the way you are
and always will be:
sailing through
the skies of Neptune,
your little glass trident
forever brandished
on our shores.

But that was last year.
If only the night
had heard us then
as we reached
for our iPhones,
the sky still filled with wonder
so long before
its mirrors
turned their backs on us,
now just reflecting
an image of the stars –

a shadow on your face
or exhibition in time,
long since faded
by your longing.

XVIII

When she played Debussy
on her custom Fazioli
I could only think
of all those men out there
in the audience
who didn't care
about the Arabesques
and only wanted
to tear her panties off
and take her right there
in front of everyone,
beneath the laughter
of the chandelier.

But then her eyes betrayed her,
telling me she wasn't lost
in the music either,
and was already thinking
of that portal to a second future
and when it would finally close,
leaving her abandoned,
strung up and gagged
like a suckling pig
in an Asian marketplace.

Drowning out the sound
of her hidden peril,
would she dare denounce
the sympathy of the Angels,

their flaming irises
too remote to even see us?
And would our own mortality
seem any less astonishing
if we could somehow
see it laid open and bare
beside them
on some preternatural screen,
their frosted wings
now flapping
in full view before us?

Her breath returns
and I am once again reminded
of those ivory keys
and the aural scent of Debussy
now ushering me
through the ceiling.
For a moment
I feel I am there amongst
them (those lofty ones)
and am sure I can even hear
their subtle voices –
the sound of a cymbal
in rich decay. Yet all I can
discern (I regret to say)
is their desperate urging
for me to tear off her panties
and take her right
then and there
beneath the laughter

of the chandelier.

XIX

The clouds – yes, the clouds!
hoarding the lavish
feast of the sky, their fat
bellies sliced open

by the bayonets of Fifth Avenue,
threatening to spill
their blood and entrails
over the beer-stained floor

of the night. It was summer
and I wandered lost
through the petroleum
fumes of subway trains,

past elegant shop windows,
alight with the sparkling whirl
of Chanel and Dior, a great anxiety
eclipsing my heart.

The World once hibernated
In your eyes, but since it wandered
from its shelter it roams
through other plains. The boats

no longer sound their horns
across dark abandoned waters
and our crows refuse
to gather in their place

outside my window. Longing
for the spectre of your
comfort, I choose instead
the ecstasy of denial,

wishing - no, demanding! - every moment
to see the clouds – yes, the clouds!
bleed out like rain, crowning
us with their bowels of shame.

XX

Let them wander through citadels of prayer
and adultery, forever
Greeted by strangers at their doors.

Let them establish their grim and fatalistic
laws in public courtrooms
Of clown fish and ocean sponges.

Let them brand the skins of monetary
jaguars, expanding their dominion
Of defunct banks and imaginary treasuries.

Let them assault us with toys and war
machines, staking their flags
In the heart of the aborted dawn.

Let them cast their secret ballots, voting on
the rights of autumn lightning
And insurrection.

Let them swim in six-star mountain spas:
thermal baths spraying their faces
With fake news and greed.

Let them stare into the mouth of the
Chimera, singing ominous ballads
of gravitational waves and teenage sex.

Let them build their exploding launch pads,
training colonies of wasps
For future missions to Mars.

Let them shop in empty boulevards for baby
carriages and Data Protection Acts,
Searching for The Devil's perfect gift.

Let them dance in the halls of enemy
nations: drugged celebrities in halcyon rags
Railing against the passage of time.

Let them drift into their ceremonial states of
trance and levitation,
Speaking in tongues on the six o'clock
news.

And we will follow them to that hidden
safehouse they promised to destroy –
And there we will stage our final conquest.

XXI

Enraptured by nothing
but the wisdom
of the birds, I strolled
into the abyss,
the forest air still yearning
for the nettle of your breath.

At the base of that pit
I could see
clearly for the first time –
the evening sky condensed into
a single star.

And when the cities receded,
their metal fountains
now a faint mirage,
I was finally alone with you,
but still alone.

How amongst the gravel
and roots can we resurrect
the breathless caravan
of those winter afternoons,
when the whole world
still reminded us
how it had fallen
from the Sun?

Licking from the paw of the lion

with tornados in our arms
we never felt the need
for danger. It was with us.
That's what I said:
we never felt the need
for danger. It wanted us.

The present returns,
a strange lacquer
hiding the grey defects
of the trees. We were
beautiful then,
we really were.

Lying in the bed beside you
when nothing mattered
but the iris in your eyes.

XXII

The death of an egoist
happens every day,
you say. Another false Diadem
swallowed up
by the marble floors
and Rothkos,
while the newspapers
said it would never happen,
with all our mighty children
still losing themselves
in their palace in the sky.

Frailty, if only you were
my adversary
and not some tiny flower
I could finally invite you
into my cellar
and offer you
that Amontillado
I always said I had –
the wet cement
still lying in a pail
somewhere out there
in the darkness.

But no, life doesn't afford us
such luxuries.
This is the modern era,
(or at least you keep saying)

where rose bushes take root
in stale cerebellums,
their thorny stems
replacing our memories
without even claiming
a bounty.

But somehow it was there,
in the heart of this frailty
where I finally found you:
naked and stretched
across our bed
in the marzipan afternoon,
your Givenchy perfume
waiting to usher me
to your palace in the sky.

XXIII

Anchored to our silence,
we alerted the medics
to supply us with oxygen

and pull us from the waters,
but no one came. So we
downloaded the App

and summoned Jupiter,
Star of the night,
to draw us into the sky.

But even he was too busy
to help us (so much for divinity).
Given the state of things,

where in the crackling
of that eternal hearth can we hear
the footsteps of those strangers

who used to circle our bed
at night? I can almost smell them
now, drenched in their stylish

aldehydes: flimsy shields
hiding us from date rapes
and random beheadings.

Or is this too big a question,

one never asks for an answer?
With so much against us,

another question now threatens
to upend us. Were we just a new
cliché thrown to the wind,

a way of diverting ourselves
from everything we really wanted
but had no means to achieve?

XXIV

For I am the lord of endless wonder, let me
line your walls with lightning and quasars,
Transforming your window into a curtain of
the stars.

For I am the builder of great railroads, let
me drive my spikes across your deserts,
My rapturous diesels roaring through the
chasm of the night.

For I am the horseman of lavender and
apocalypse, let me lift my dreaded cowl
To reveal my tearful infant eyes.

For I am the architect of silence and dawn,
let me build my woollen viaducts
Across the frozen causeways of your
longing.

For I am the jester of the almond night, let
me juggle my graphene corncobs
On your unicycles of rubber and nails.

For I am the merchant of shellfish and
redemption, let me scatter my crimson
pearls
Through the COVID of your shame.

For I am the blacksmith of eternal hope, let
me hammer my neon horseshoes
On your anvils of deception.

For I am the flower tranquilized beneath
your bed, let me awaken at last
To pollinate the terror of your dreams.

For I am the Admiral of forgotten summers,
let me guide my blissful warships
Through your oceans of regret.

For I am the accountant of numerology and
love, let me balance your scandalous tax
sheets In the Pentagon of my forgiveness.

For I am the lost imprisoned child, let me
escape your shores of ivory and Novichok,
Laughing and forever free.

Forget you ever heard these words, and
rampage with your diamond lances,
Sharpened for the endless night.

Other Poems
(2021-22)

The Crescendo

Fleeting moments expand like tongues
of fire into the throat of my words,
your sword revealed in an instant –
withdrawn from the sheath of your eyes.

But soon the night called us, its ivy
creeping through our open windows
where no bird sings and shadows
of your past are still starving for my love.

When the winter came your breath
protected us, but the snow passed
its own laws, chiselled on abandoned
roads and desolate tree trunks

Where there – yes, *there* – you became one
and I became the other, and we both
became nothing but that which vanished
in those words, once spoken but now lost

In the tarnished night, where even the stars
refuse
to dance in the evening's rapturous
crescendo.

The Pool

In the middle of a forest
I came across a pool
and threw a stone in it,
but there were no ripples

And when I looked
into the stillness
the only reflection
I could see was your face
staring out at me
with your hopeful eyes

And it made me realize
that you are my reflection
and that no matter which
stone I throw, you will
always bring me calm

And that you must also
inhabit a dark forest
somewhere with its own
pool, perhaps a different
shape, colour, or depth,

And when you throw a stone
in it there are also no ripples
when my face stares back
at you as you search
for your reflection.

This pool is our love
and it shines on forever,
through the wanton
rampage of the day
or the quiet lunar night,
fusing our souls together
as we walk through
the gates of eternity.

The Cinnamon Tree

Where in that ancient cymbal
hiss can we still discern
the gilded summons
of that lost reverb trail
that once was our bannister,
guiding us through
uncharted days,
now growing longer
than the breath
of their own shadow?

Or is it just the thought
of a cinnamon tree
that haunts me,
when I cannot even verify
that cinnamon comes from trees,
having never wandered
far enough down the path
of that particular search term,
which always ends,
I imagine, in the origin
of all thought?

So, follow me down
those empty paths,
through unspoken words
and blank Google pages,
now just murmuring voices
echoing in quadrants

where even the sultry thrush
has forgotten how to fly
and there we will find
each other in our purest form:
two broken bells
waiting to be struck
in the vernal song
of their own emptiness.

When I opened the curtains
the day somehow greeted us
before the dawn was even visible,
speaking in its own Brail –
a language I am blind to
just as a blizzard is blind
to the motions of a clock
or the pain it inflicts
on us teachers of children,

Or the joy it brings
to those same children
still waiting for the snow.

The Labyrinth

I built myself a labyrinth to protect me from
your eyes, but its carbon fibre walls soon
proved too thin to conceal my whereabouts,
thus allowing the minotaur to cease its
random wanderings and sharpen its horns
for a final attack.

But still your gaze was everywhere, and
even though the minotaur spared my life
with a muffled snort and begrudging stab of
its horns, I was left in a pool of my own
blood, crying for salvation beneath the
blanket of your shadow.

My strength redoubled by self-contempt, I
escaped the labyrinth and took shelter in the
eyes of infants, drinking great Burgundies in
marble executive suites furnished with the
finest ottomans, while newspaper syndicates
collapsed from lack of readership, social
media went mute, and new internet sites
were born from nothing, advertising
redemption in the form of pastoral
symphonies composed by rap stars.

Eventually I hid out in a linoleum cellar of
my own design. I listened to rock bands
consisting only of women with ocean green
hair. I bought land in the arctic and sold

shoes at a loss until eventually I finished
five-hundredth in a lottery, winning just
enough to pay my bills and hide from you
for yet another winter.

Spring came without warning and I was
suddenly lost again in my labyrinth. It was
as though the retreat of the minotaur had
been an illusion all along. I quickly took
refuge in the centre of the maze, where I was
certain I would be safe from your eyes.

But there was a television screen on the wall
I never noticed before, announcing a new
scandal of Watergate proportions where key
politicians had lied to the people, their
advisors, and even themselves.

I heard the minotaur breathing somewhere in
the distance and on the television the police
suddenly started tear gassing themselves
instead of the angry rioters. It was
something nobody quite understood, but
everyone could see so clearly before them:

The end of my solitude and the beginning of
our love.

Ballad of a Retired Man

I worked for a mummy once –
he was my boss for much of my life

and his odour was made no less repugnant
by the frankincense his wife insisted he use,

or his bandages made less visible
through the lens of his grey Macey's suit.

Now I am retired and have saved enough
To finally build a house, with a pool

In the backyard and vines crawling
Up the clinker brick walls

My boss died many years ago, leaving
His wife alone to whither in their
condominium

And while he had never once visited me
In my backyard, I can still see his eyes

Glaring at me through the sycamores,
And I wonder if he is happy for me

At last, or if he thinks my new house
Is really his, having paid me every penny

I saved along the way to build it. It's a
question
That will trouble me until I eventually find

My way beneath the dirt in my own
backyard,
Perhaps to join him once again in his lost
pyramid.

The Fig Tree (for René Char)

Death of all midnight, eclipsed
By the fig tree of her kisses,
When the starlight is no longer

A forest, and her tunnel of darkness
Is suddenly closed to all outsiders,
Her curls now trampled by the silence

Of her pillowcase. Drunk on the sap
of the moment, we reach out to the eternal
Song, which always demands we elude it.

Oh, never! When stone walls surround us
And time shrinks to a blood-stained pinhead,
Will we ever find you in the light of dawn?

The Kite

If I were lost
somewhere
in the middle
of the wind,

the dark sky
crushing down
on my back –
a deadly piano

without a tune –
blinded there
by the hood
of the rain,

I would search
its slippery keys
for a memory
of you and me

somewhere
in Sao Paulo
before the dark
ages returned,

and tether it
to a string,
setting it loose
behind the clouds:

a Chinese kite,
lifting us
above the rain
into the depths

of the azure sky.

Grey Light

Grey light, who are you?

I first embraced you in an alleyway only to
abandon you that very night with nothing
but the wind to sustain you.

I saw you in pools of rain on highway
shoulders and in the mirage of empty shop
windows, I heard you in the basements of
department stores; I tasted your lips as I
watched you in the pulsing mirrored floor of
an East-end nightclub, grooming your
coiffured hair.

I observed you in the eyes bankers as they
exit elevators on the forty-first floor of some
office tower, scrutinizing documents I no
longer have.

I married you at midnight when your gown
was stained and a crippled child stood as
witness, and when we divorced a week later
there were no clouds in the sky, but the
horizon was the colour of your tears.

You radiate from lamp posts, singing the
Devil's chorus from the gas flame of my
stove and I feel you in the light of dawn

when my bedsheets still reek of your
cologne.

Grey light, we are bound by infinity, but
only in death can I find you.

The Bridge

I saw you on a bridge
one day,

a flower balanced in your hair,

the wind casting
its own favourable
judgement
by letting it stay there,
undisturbed.

And when I reached out
to touch it,
you touched my hand
instead, and smiled:

too late for eternity?

It could have been Paris
Or Singapore, or maybe
Milan or Marrakech

that wasn't the important
thing. It was the way
you touched my hand
and let me wrap my finger
around yours

while you smiled even

more strongly, letting
us freezeframe the moment

there on the bridge

when the wind
with all its immortal
kindness, made sure
the flower stayed there,

balanced in your hair.

Jesus

I caught a glimpse of Jesus
once, lurking behind
the flugelhorn
in a Kreuzberg bar
before the lights blinked on
and we were all asked
to finish our drinks
and leave.

That night I was sure
He was standing there
between the light
and shadow cast
by the puce draperies
of my hotel room,
a woman naked
and sleeping on the bed,
asking for nothing
nor demanding nothing:
the Sun itself
crucified by the midnight sky.

When nothing but the Spring
is there to save us
what do we really see,
but all those things
that conspire to destroy us –
the bridges of our minds
traversing that river

we can never cross?

Yet, all the while,
the radiant sound
of a fluegelhorn
still transfigures
the smoky air.

In the Shadow of Morning

Fires of mist:
the breath of morning
calling a bomb squad
to my window.

Clouds of diamond
cutting through
the dawn: the teeth
of a laith.

Trees of frost,
their drooping boughs
immersing my days in shadow:
the hourglass of your loss.

Eyes of starlight
towering over my bed:
their cold white light
the executioner of my dreams.

Lips of silence
bending over my trembling eyelids:
their Chapstick aftertaste
a court summons for the day

That never seems to come.

Song of Ruin

You, who walk through bitter canyons
where only the blackest flowers are free
from the deadly pulse of the cartographer

charting yet newer constellations in drifts
of brown snow, walk with me this hour
of grief, the swansong of the sacred smelter

now lost to centuries of ruin. Touching
your aching hand to soothe its blood blisters,
would it be any different than today?

If only we had walked together sooner,
or watched the traffic lights, strolling
through
the ending's many moods, maybe then that
song

would still be tossing its embers into our
ears.

Paula

I found you, little dancer
behind a blade of frozen grass,

the candles in your eyes
providing warmth to all vision

and your siren's voice
inviting the world to feast

inside my special illusion,
cast across the sky

with amphetamine clarity
as though to muffle

the shooting of the stars.
But when the freight train

swallowed you,
its sharp iron teeth

tearing you asunder,
you rose into the sky

cradled by the smoke
of its diesel turbine.

My ears almost bleeding
from the screeching

of its breaking wheels
you looked down upon me

and cast your spell once more,
from behind that blade

of frozen grass
now swaying in the sky.

In a Metro Station

One night I was engulfed by the saffron
glow of a streetlamp, and a hole opened
inside me, exploding through my soul with
the ferocity of mushroom cloud.

In mortal fear, I took refuge in the rain,
concealing myself behind the droplets,
veiled by the clouds of humidity rising from
the pavement.

In my hidden bunker I listened to music,
training my ear to the sound of infinity. I
danced - a whirling dervish fused with the
glassy perfection of a ballerina - as I
devoured tomes of great philosophy, all
vacuous in the face of this new menace
inside me.

I studied gravitational waves and divined the
future in the patterns of cyclones. I dined
with elegant statesmen on meals of venison
and hyena.

Flowers bloomed inside me and I died a
thousand times before a single petal fell.
Clouds billowed through the night, invisible,
yet screaming wild incantations that I was
certain only I could hear.

Then one clear morning I saw you in the
Metro station, *a petal on a wet black bough*
already too tired a metaphor to describe you
as you emerged from the train.

Seeking to elude you, I retreated further into
the rain, inventing formulas for new alloys
with properties of levitation of matter and
storage of infinite energy, resistant to even
the heat of the Sun.

But you were still there in the Metro, staring
at me, demanding a response I could not
give because the hole inside me was
growing larger with every passing moment,
threatening to consume me like an infinite
nightmare.

I heard you in the wheels of cars, in the
sound of branches swaying in the wind, in
the chorus of gravestones elevated from the
dying earth.

Wherever I went I only saw your reflection
in my mirror. I taught myself the piano, the
flute, the lyre, and played symphonies on the
back of a comb.

Adorned in rags, I slept in boxes and spoke
to rats and mosquitos. I lived on slices of

toast smeared with expired marmalade for weeks on end.

But the hole only grew wider and deeper. Fearing my tragic end, I collapsed in anguish on the granite floors of the Metro station.

But when I turned to look up, I saw you staring over my shoulder. "I am not who you think I am," you said. "And every time you retreat further from me, you will only lose yourself even more than you already have. I followed you through your paths of darkness and plunged with you into the deepest wells of your despair."

"Can't you just leave me alone?" I pleaded.

But even as these words left my mouth, I felt for the first time I was flying through her emerald eyes on a pair of gifted wings that only she had the power to revoke.

In a sudden epiphany, I realized she really was Ezra Pound's *petal on* a *wet black bough*, only I was too blind and cowardly to see it.

So, I said, becoming more sheepish by the moment (certain my words were pretentious

and ridiculous as soon as I uttered them):
"Rescue me from my prison of loneliness,
and let me fly with you on your emerald
chariot."

And with these words the hole finally
receded, as though Hiroshima was reborn
from the ashes in some miraculous reverse
explosion.

I took your hand and walked with you to the
escalator leading down to the Metro
platform. Against the background rumble of
an incoming train, "We forgot to buy our
tickets," was all I heard you say.

White Flower

Where amongst my demons
Can I find you, white flower?

In the bland triumph of escalators
And the city's longitudinal cafés,

Or those secret summer hideaways
We once threw to the shadows,

All now bleeding out in time,
Your poison seeping from my veins?

Pan's Orchard

Floating freely through life's scandal,
Adorned with the neckless of the ages,
I suckle the abandoned breast

Of those who once witnessed us,
Feigning to inhale the spiral air
That always kept us buoyant,

As we ascend their hidden staircase
Where we can once again watch
The sway of the ocean's tides – singing.

Words echo through ancient corridors,
always
Asking "what is it?" or "where will it be?"
And "why are you not me, or me you?"

Or "are these questions not the same,
Or somehow very different from that which
was
Just once and never will be again?"

If only your lips could play that lost oboe,
Breathing the songs that once were our
shadow
Cast as if by some invisible umbrella

Onto the pavement's dull chorus, as I posed
There as Icarus, raging in your lap, or errant

Pan spellbound in your orchard.

But how can we unfold an undrawn map,
Or wander through a garden never planted
No matter how our paths failed to cross?

For when I finally return, I will have already
left
And when we come together (forever and at
last)
I will no longer be there, nor anywhere at
all.

Frank Capra

When our dreams
come true at last
I will be in black and white
and you will too,
in an old movie
where everything always
seems to work out
and the world
is a happy place
where all the villains
get what they deserve.
I will look deeply
into your eyes
and a violin will play
when I kiss you
and when I sweep
you off your feet
the orchestra will hit
in a wave of emotion,
a crescendo
like none before,
and the audience will cry
into their handkerchiefs.
When the credits
start to role
and people file
towards the exits,
already eager
to see us again

and tell the world
how great we were
in the magical
story of our love
and about everything
we fought against
and triumphed
to make our dreams
come true.
But when they leave
the theatre
and catch a taxi home
through the rain
the windshield wipers
will have already
made them forget,
reminding them instead
about setting the alarm
for tomorrow morning
and what new things
the next workday
might bring.

The Promise

Since I met you
oranges fill the sky
and there is music
playing in my head –
a carnival in my dreams
where rabbits chase
the fox away
to a place in the forest,
trees smoothing
their branches
in the wind,
once a raging storm
but now just
a forgotten song.

"In Prague anything is possible,"
a stranger said, their voice
quickly drowned amongst the pigeons.

Little promise
star of promises,
pencil hidden
between the sheets,
our nightlight
voicing the glory
of pure silence,
when will your breath
return us to the morning's
custody, erasing

whatever darkness
still wets the rims
of your eyes?

I once took your hand and kissed it:
all black water lost
in the eyes of the Danube,
the castle staring down
from the sky.

Where in this silence
can I find you,
Your face a pattern
in the snow
and your voice
the sound of my finger
composing music
on the edge of a glass?

Perhaps some Spring day
I will meet you
in the rain,
the blades of grass
leaning from
their dew of guilt,
or hear your voice
in the call of a meditating crow
perched on some broken fence
in the cold touch of *now*.

No matter how invisible,

I feel you every moment
in the hollow knocking of the day
or the warm sting of night,
always knowing
that when we meet again
I will touch your hand –

all black water forever lost
in the eyes of the Danube.

To An Unknown Woman

When Picasso
first painted a lily
or Van Gogh
a meteor
lighting up
the Paris skies
could they ever
have known
something infinitely
more beautiful
would ever exist,
so beautiful
that no painter
could ever do it justice?
And if they were
resurrected
in Madrid or Paris
some scattershot day
in the summer heat
how would they even
begin to erect
their easels
and start painting
your eyes
or your smile,
surrounded
by that radiant cloud
that is our love?
No matter what

they painted,
they would give up
in frustration
only to start over again –
so used to making
a rose look better
than a rose,
until the end
of eternity,
because this time
they will have met
their match:
you and your love
are too beautiful
for any painter
to even try.

But no matter
how many times
I try to catch your eye
to tell you this,
you just turn
and walk away.

The Death of Man Ray

White grains
On black celluloid
A flower burns
Like a tiny star
Etching its way
Into nothingness

You always had
A leg up on me –
Posing for the world
In bright stockings,
While I tried to write
The perfect letter

From the other side
Of the world. But lately
A woman I no longer
Love sits throned
In her private Orient:
The death of Man Ray.

The Searcher (for Leonard Cohen)

I searched for you
In white pagodas
Dreamed into your eyes,
But found instead
Those Guardians of silence
Bound by an eternal game
They've long since forgotten.

I craved for you
In midnight songs
Numbed onto the floor,
My desperate pen
Crying for the ink
Of tears I once wished for
But never came.

I swam for you
In volcanic springs,
Drenched in the vigour
Of your lips,
As we rained down
From imaginary clouds
Now lost to the sky.

I wandered for you
Through the heart of Jesus
My bleeding feet
Hidden from the Stranger's eye –
Hate at my back,

Until I finally found you there:
So naked on my cross.

Early Poems
(1980-1986)

Hymns to Light

I

Poetry is simple fire. From the other side
Of the thread the vacant light moves through
The eye of the shimmering needle.

II

To ascend, to climb into the starry light,
Beyond these walls, beyond these very
words,
To free my pupils from the bread which
stands
Upon the floor.

III

Alas, I am of another clay, molded in
strange forms
Whose twisted cycles I cannot decode,
whose furious colors
You see before me.

IV

Clear, like the silence of a flower, this
mirror
Stands as always. The hair I see is dark, the
eyes

I see are gold.

V

When I look upon the streets they seem to
be a maxim,
Reduced to the bare possibilities of
grammar, declensions
On a yellowed page.

VI

Beautiful, she's rising, like Lucifer or
Micha-el,
Into the surging air, radiating light she
cannot understand,
Nor wants to understand. Softly I succumb.

VII

Poetry is silence. The space between these
words
Is the space between these blazing worlds.
Bright, and vibrating
Slowly to some vast rhythm.

VIII

The harbor lights roll so slowly through

The blackish air, circle on circle moving
towards
The empty pier.

IX

Pale, like the blue globe of morning,
She rests her sleepy head.
Is everything a finer light reflecting
Off yet finer hands?

X

But the streetlight feels its cruel yellow
Glow and the city is so strong and cold.

XI

Her whitened palms caress me beneath the
shoulder
Of the dawn.
Kneel, oh Lord, to the handiwork of hands,
kneel
Into the summit of your light.

XII

Can the cage which keeps the bird bend and
curl
Until it seems like water shining on her silky
wings?

XIII

To Hell with it! these women. Their faces
Are a fifth appendage and their smiling fills
the air
With *spleen*. How should I feel blessed
For this cynic's disposition? Should I die at
last,
Consumed within this arctic Hell?
Feeling thus is perdition on its own.

XIV

Listen, young child, to the deadly ripple
Of the tide.
Fill your ears with wonder, the salacious
Humming of the sea.
Dance about in the cold white sand, and you
will
Feel the power.
The surging of mute water through your
chalky toes.

XV

And.

XVI

Thus, I sing to light. Oh,

Rise, burn, flare, and singe.
Return to the image of the star-washed
Night. Poetry is this rupture, this rising,
This conflagration
In the valleys of all sight.

Lyon 1982

Fatal, she listens to the slow fall
Of waves on morning stone,
And her thighs move gently through
The air inside her dress.

Unreal, oh vision! The hot Sun scraping
Through the shapeless Lyon sky.
The mountain, the cathedral
The elephant. Striped umbrellas

In open lanes, and lizards
Decorate the tiles
Of porches and verandas
On a humid August day.

But, still the longing for the mountain
And the skin beneath her dress.

The Death of Sardanapalus

I

A flash of bright color,
The tangled nudes upon
the floor,
And not even an Angel's cruel hand
Could cut through the violent
beauty
Of the collapsing light,
As he watched his eager soldiers
Slit the soft, warm
throats
Of his drunken concubines.
 Muffled screams deflected off indifferent
walls
While the hot winds
peeled shingles
From the burning towers.
It wasn't like the Massacre at Scio, no,
Where scores of innocent
men
Were casually
condemned
To the selfish whims of the Sun,
Helplessly crumpled on the
golden sands
Waiting for that final sound
In the quiet beauty
Of God's final thrust.

II

        No, not at all.
Sardanapalus sat lazily awaiting his death
          As he watched the red-
wet fingers
    Drench his linen sheets
       Almost enjoying the way
         The blood seemed to
shine
     Behind a thin veil of opium
       Lost within his own
      Half-crazed light, weakly
yearning
    For another's silent grace.

III

     Yes, in that moment he became
Delacroix,
        Standing loosely in his
damp studio
Painting the strong black bodies
     While naked girls
        Pulled freshly picked
flowers
    From their flowing hair
      Watching as the artist's
        Delicate hands
pulled

Even his face from Death's
pale garden
As if it needed to gaze
With more fabulous eyes
At the oily brush which laid beside the
broken
Easel.

A Soul's Breath

Montreal is a hymn
To the open river
With grey-green Jaguars
And a cross that lights the hill.
Not a moment's peace
Save for those Portuguese sandals
And the expensive but sour wine
Which populates the purple shops
Like mussels on the Brighton sand.
Black haired girls
Walk into *Za Za*
La la la
Breathing a soul's breath
In this sea of colored shoes
And cinematic dreams
One begins to pray
That Heraclitus will rise
From the river soon.

Evening in the City

I

This city! The very rudeness of its
ignorance!
The buses at noon, a woman cradling her
groceries
like and infant with diarrhea. What insipid
memories! I pass a Chinese furniture shop.
Hah! A wicker monkey, a stuffed Macaw, I
can
only laugh, sneering is too blunt, just like
this place.

Again it is night. I walk across a lonely
bridge as the moon casts its pale vapor
throughout
the hollow street and I stare into the languid
purple
river fuming below me. It reminds me of
defection. I
think of Alchemy: glistening metal tubes,
obscure
symbols, vials filled with bubbling fluids.
Never,
never before have I been so thus
consumed…

The confused babbling of life annoys me in

every aspect. Things will not orient
themselves,
they're always shifting. Man, merely man,
even my
Angels seem frightening in their awesome
beauty.
Leave me alone! I prefer the company of
less
obnoxious guests, thieves and rapists would
please me more. "But remember, David,
you can't
mistrust…" Bah! Who needs the Logos,
the scented
candles; the charms. Perhaps I shall die
miraculously
someday, frozen in an Arctic Hell, never to
be
found!

II

Dawn scatters her pointed crystals across the
river's surface, awakening me as they
stretch into
the darkness, defining it. I feel the
extrication,
I am a speckled bird, free to fly over any hill
I
may; I am raptured by my radiance…

Born into an urban family (there were only

complexities) I quickly learned to hate the beautiful,
as it mocked the ugly, and of course, we were the
ugly, a few gnarled stumps amongst the thriving
junipers.

I look into the light again, I can no longer
distinguish it from the shadows that it forms. I
perceive not beauty, but ugliness as it shines like
plated jewelry or maybe cheap crystal. Is every
experience like this? Can no one find a center?

Summer

Summer, its whips,
Its pillars, its lions.
And long faces crowd
The death of flowers
In its hot, nagging boulevards.
Open, its cities, its hostels
Its restaurants
Where bald sailors
Spit, and chew
Their fatty meat,
Where leather sandals wind
Up the legs of thin virgins
And waitresses wait
For better wages.

Summer, its mosques
Its tiles, its elephants.
And the fat Algerian,
Who points his knife
At your face and then your wallet,
Grins while smoke leaks
Through his yellow teeth.
Dark, its alleys, its sewers,
Its mind.
And perfumed ladies
Walk the streets like soldiers
Of the night, decorated
With memories
Of another past.

Soon it will be gone
As water falls through an open funnel,
As words fall from an open mouth.
Stripped of winter's fantasy,
I turn and fall asleep.

To André Bretton

The oval silence
Which burns my ears
Rises into being –
The Earth returns,
Stone!
This creature that I serve
Breaks clear windows
In stale kitchens
And the craving that
I feel
Rises into Being –
The Earth returns,
Stone!
Capable of nothing,
Fingers colder than
The eyes of fat men,
Seen only by dark statues
And you,
I watch the vague growth
Of indolence
From within my wooly womb,
And it rises into being –
The Earth returns,
Stone!

Late Fall

I was born, cold, dark, inhuman, killing
Every stranger's stare.

And that's how I died, in this grey
Stone prison, devouring each scrap of light
Like a rabid dog slouching in the alleys of
the night.

The Sun drooped low and tired calves
squatted
Beneath a golden yew tree, and the Earth
ground slowly around its graphite
axis.

But suddenly! A ribbon of light and already
The orange-grey glow of winter rubs me
with its virgin
Warmth.

Insouciant cats prowl through the grinning
street,
Insolent, unwilling to succumb to their
keeper's scolding
Glare.

And children revel in the red and yellow
leaves,
Smiles in the red and yellow leaves: boots,
black

With red soles, cries, blond hair –
And breezes in the cold of a cloudless sky.

Never will a moment reveal such an infinity
of other
Moments, and never will an orange and
yellow leaf
Reflect such a cradle of possibilities.

I walk, awakened, through the reddened ivy
halls
While leaves hand loosely from their naked
branches
Like tiny marionettes, thinking of that
hardened prison
And if it shall return.

For a Certain Lady

Quelle est l'heure?
I've been dead for weeks,
Or, at least, wildly drunk
For a day, but you?

Your hair is so thin
And your skull stares so rudely
Through those pretty cheeks.
Perhaps my eyes are lying,

They get so bored just sitting
In their little holes. Where
Have you been? A night in the rain?
By the bridge? In someone else's garden?

Her shoes softly glisten,
Stabbing holes in dirty puddles
As she turns and walks away.

Koksidje-Bad

Lord, make still your chalky hands, withdraw
Your quiet soldiers

And their wounded squires, let me sleep in tents
Of Sabine women,

Deep inside the Roman walls, where only the smell
Of fresh-cut linen

Fills the morning air. Return your tired horses
To their mossy stables

And hang your rusted armor on the empty walls.
For, life's fierce battle

Has me weary since love has gone away.

Cities of Light

I. City of the Merchants

Cold city,
City of loneliness, City of the moon,
Where fallen souls wander through yawning
streets,
Submerged in emptiness, yearning for the
miracle
of Death.
City: poised in lapidary silence like a
gargoyle
At dawn, breveting its weary prey.
Pallid city, suffused in grey smoke
Under the light of a tiring moon,
City at the lunar hour, hung between
The fear of exile
And the nightmare of freedom,
Inhaling an ambience of fog
On a chilled, deserted night –
And the rain whipped pavement,
The breath of smog aloft,
The hearts of those within her,
Sordid,
Limber,
Soft.

II. Of the Rain

Ah, but the rain moves so smoothly

Through the dripping alleyways,
Curling through the musty hollows,
Whirling through reposing eddies,
Reaching further,
Further back,
Into the corners of yet deeper pools –
And already the scent of myrrh
Mingles in the chambers of your dreams.

III. The Dream Sequence

The granite gaze of horned beasts
importuning
The speckled night; tower, auger of the
heavens,
Constructed in stone and hammered brass,
with
Crumbling steps ascending to a tiered arch,
and
Below, a profusion of ancient cloths
embroidered
In threads of bronze and azure: looming
halls, the
Scent of salt and strange perfumes drifting
Through the midnight air: Frankincense and
bitter
Musk; lavender oils and hyacinth balms, yet
sweeter
Mists, burned with slender candles at the
invocation

Of Ya. Elder, cloaked in white, wearing
sandals
Of dried milk: Initiate of the Linking Cubes.

IV. Of the Revelation

"Oh Exile!
Your stony beasts are not more hated, nor
Their heavy breath more despised: but I
Have seen them, oh wise merchants, (I
Have seen myself redeemed!) have seen
them
From the lofty tiers of knowledge with
Their granite manes and brazen claws,
smothering
Your every flitting thought, like a salient
Thundercloud, gnawing at the margins
Of the day.
And every hour you sink deeper into
The grinding jowls of your mangy lives!
Blind merchants!
Your wicker monkeys and stuffed macaws
Know nothing of the gargoyles, nor of
The fragrant halls of incense, which
They eternally conceal from the eyes
Of striving outcasts, beneath the thickness
Of the rolling fog."

The Bells of St. Michael's

It is time to ascend,
Beyond this room,
Beyond these walls
Beyond this wary city.
The ringing of the bells
Fills the footpaths of my soul.
Shop windows,
Streetlights, busses,
And the sacred flower
Which rolls into the hidden light
All come together,
Are reborn,
By the steps of St. Michael's
On this all-enchanted
God-befriended day.
The alleys frame this vision
Like a fresco,
Seeming to seem or not to seem
To ghostly or ashamed.

Paris Spleen

The buildings are capped in warm brown
snow
And all of the boulevards are aflame with
the ariel
Light and romance of a post-war night.

Schoolgirls with rouged cheeks and long
wool
Coats pull their lovers scarves and laugh at
their
Worn out shoes. What fatal passion, oh
ecstasy
Of the icy streets!

Soldiers fight the brawling drunks and
photos
Gleam in front of flashing theaters
frequented
By the filthy rich. Oh, pain and agony of
this cozy
City shining like a dripping dagger.

Godlessness, and what ripe visions on this
day
Of hours, this hour of days, the minutes
falling
Through my frostbit fingers.

And I, the not I, stand aimlessly, rubbing milky
Shoulders with the endless night.

The Chinese Mummers

Through my window I can see,
Now, as at every hour of these humid nights,
Those grinning mummers,
Their arms flailing through the dark black
air
Their eyes gleaming like tiny marbles
Beneath the neon glow,
And their slippered feet moving in hidden
patterns
Across the joyous street.

There! Her hand, seductive, passes
Over his rigid coiffured hair and across
His painted face, calmly
He turns his head in gesture towards
The chalk-white moon.

Enraptured in their lovers' dance,
Enfeebled by this lunar trance
They jump and drink to some new God
Who rules the world of risk and chance.

My Metro

I walk onto my metro
There are faces on my metro
Long, thin faces and long
Thin fingers clutching crumpled
Papers near oily windowpanes.
My metro follows winding
Tunnels through cities
Through lives and deaths and
Through the vengeance wanting
Death.
There is light upon my metro
Reflecting off of shiny doors
Into the eyes of fat men who
Face the silence of walls
Who know the silence of facing
Walls, standing frozen waiting
For something like a stop
Perhaps the next or perhaps
Some other, gazing at the empty
Walls.
Babies cry on my metro.
Mothers comfort babies crying
On my metro, feeding them
Milk or feeding them some
Ugly trepidation,
Lost in labyrinths, lost in thought,
Waiting, waiting for Alexandria,
Waiting for Babylon,, waiting
For the thin silence

Of early morning stations,
Waiting for fried eggs
In early morning stations.
There are flowers on my metro,
Graves and flowers in an ecstasy
Of blood, there are flowers
On my metro,
Falling in bouquets from
Florescent ceilings, falling,
Falling through the glowing
Air into the fatal mouths of tunnels
Feeling sickness in the mouths
Of fatal tunnels, always dying
In the mouths of fatal tunnels.

Bristol, 1972

I'm waiting for the airy hands of God
To blow into my room,
For the Japanese sock kites to fly above
The colorful umbrellas,
And for René Char to open he belated
Christmas present.
I'm waiting for St. Michael, St. Thomas
And St. Catherine
To walk into my dusty room, and for that
little
Piece of taffy
That you have inside your purse. I'm
waiting
For a lamb's death,
But that little girl on the bridge says I may
Be waiting forever.

Angels in the Street

No one but the Angels
Could see you now,
Hands clamping your face
In subhuman ecstasy,
Eyes burnt through like
Worn out batteries as you
Glare through those pillar-like
Fingers into the violent light
Of birth.
No, not even your most shining
Mystics could peer into the crystal
Of your most errant heart.
Bodies scattered across the dusty
Street,
Lovers, those pretty mirrors,
Languorous upon the velvet couch
Of evening,
Faces avoiding all true direction,
Preferring to admire glass towers
Or maybe just a shiny car.
No, no one but the Angels
(their hair is like fire) could
Penetrate the mystery
of your most errant heart
(we move like glass slippers through
Their gentle hands).

Psalm

Behind my eyes there burns
A heartless flame,
Behind my heart there burns
The Cosmic Sun
And through my mind there moves
The starry shapes of night.
But Orpheus, child of light,
Who are these spirits
Whose eyes I meet
Beyond the cool shimmer of picture
Windows?
And who is their maker (he sees
Without eyes like a charwoman
Sees through broken glass)?
Their words reveal my mystery
And their light illumines
All paradox, yet from my
Clearest mind they flow
Like tiny droplets into the whirling
Pools of morning.

Poem to a Foreign Lady

Cry in vain beneath the supple light,
Walk on porches, through snow
Or with thin rings of ivory
Dangling from your wrists.
Break me with a newer heart,
For since you have returned
My eyes gaze towards the red-stone houses
And snow falls gently on my darkened face.

Sorrow of Youth

Oh, Sorrow,
Sorrow of my youth dissolved by age
Sorrow of exotic nights
Touched by the hot mouths of ecstasy,
I remember you,
You!
From lurid days, released into the jungles
Of memory to peck apart my heart like
A brightly feathered bird with scarlet eyes
And narrow, slanted wings
That feeds upon the warm pulp
Of mangos.
My youth was that of white hands
Gliding as a neural breeze across
My happy arms
And my palate was stung by a mouth
Of wet cotton while lying amongst the girls
On grassy slopes.
We all rejoiced in laughter at those
Girls, subtle, yet clothed in striped
Dresses which even lured the wind
Beneath their skin –
Those misty eyes alluring softened
Stares in empty halls,
Those dangling sounds, weaving through
The clamor of wet leaves
Into a harem of ivory throats.
Youth!
If I could only breath your creamed cotton

Once more.

Greece, 1985

Pure incandescence!
Crumbling church bells
Call me to their feet,
And golden-white sands
Ring in the temple's
Ancient morning –
And again, I climb the mountain's
Milky thighs
With almost a breeze
Combing through its tawny
Mane,
Just waiting for the Pastor's
Word,
To warp that ring
Around your heart.

Aion

Through my doors I hear
The banners flapping through the air.
And opened, now, to the eyes of morning
I am waiting for that first consciousness
To rustle through my hair
Like a boy waiting to dive
Into the salt-foamy sea.
Tired of the cafés and scarves,
The endless whistle of streetcars
And the corners of my room
I no longer need the evening's
Loving moments
To sanctify my life.
And hence I have come to Aion,
As I walk beside this sled
Or watch another car streaming
Towards New England.

Ondine

Reaching light!
The gleaming of reflected stars.
Tiny feet, silky hands,
And a quick look of reckless glee
Move behind the shadows of the moon.
"Come with me and you can be a fish,
A branch, a stone.
Feel the warmth of my lips
And hear the whispers of the endless sand.
We can be as jewels in a precious stone
Or perfume in the angry wind."
The murky waters bend around her sultry
Light, devouring the twilight shapes
That vanish in the night.

Brighton, 1972

I

As I walk beside this salt-caked lighthouse, along
This ocean path,
The grey-white clouds affect a simple
Heaven, tiered
Above the jagged sea.
I think of Cromwell and his heady men,
King Charles
Before the blade,
Bristol, Newark, Brighton, and London
under flame.
My childhood
Had its own way, breathing in its own air,
conquering
More violent lands.
It is another history, like the first, yet
trapped
In the garden
Of its own becoming, ever lonely because it
cannot
Be shared.
And how many friends rejoiced in talk of
that first
Victory,
Or Paris in the underground? Violence is
pure action

And hence
A form of love.

II

Thus, the thinker is the cruelest man, bereft
of subtle
Contact,
And human only in flesh or duty. And
poetry is his penance
His way of returning
From the icefields or making up for June.
And our history,
This history,
Is made to settle down.

III

The thousand barges flap about on the cold
and tarry
Waves, churning towards
The anxious shores. And thoughts recede,
sinking
Into the November
Smoke, which rises from the Parliament,
now childhood
Can really settle down.

A Ghost Walks Here Tonight

A ghost walks here tonight,
His ankles are damp
With the slime of two millennia
And his toes slip loosely
Through thin gravel on stone floors.
Yet he walks, a spirit of some vague
Mission, through ivy covered buildings
And rows of wooden pews
Whispering sweet nothings
Into our deafened ears.

Two thousand years dead
His body rots to threads
On slabs of cracking Beachwood,
And his bones run cold.
Two thousand years, but hardly
Two millennia, for resurrection
Began immediately, ignoring all concern
With ancient ritual
Transfigured life upon a cross
Beneath the glowing moon.

Hidden from a vision of such providence
The gentle yew trees bend beneath the glory
Of the Sun.

Lennon's Dead

Not fist nor cross
Could raise the blood
That forty years
Laid in the mud

His body dies amongst us
A thousand shattered voices
That barely left his mouth
Float quietly through the fog.
Liverpool, Amsterdam, New York
And black vinyl discs in strangely
Colored cardboard sleeves
Decorate our shelves.
Consumed. A picture on the wall
From some naïve age.

But still the lady cries, leaning
Delicately over the piano stool
Staring into her mirror
Thinking of what it all should mean
Not really knowing the violence of Time
Or the agony of its song.
Perhaps she will wander through a garden
Some rain-eaten day and understand it all,
To understand amongst the garden birds
Is everyone's true wish
Since childhood's first fall.

Not fist nor cross

Could break the words
That forty years
Never heard.

His voice still breathes amongst us
Ringing through the smoke
In a crowded bar, burning
In the mind of that immortal street
Flattened by the late March cold.
Macy's, Harrods, Sacks
And shiny vials of perfume
Stand like tiny castles
On hills of rayon gloves.

But still the lady cries, turning
Towards the whispers of the snow
Leaking through the windowpane
Thinking of what it all had meant
Not really seeing that twelve leopards
Strung around an Asian vase
Will raise the floor at Sotheby's
But can't change the fact
That man was bought and hence
Must be returned
To that glowing kiln
And that nicely polished urn.

Not fist nor cross
Can warm the breasts
That touched against
His darkened chest.

To T. S. Eliot

The trembling leaves upon the wall
Fretfully clutching their frightened stems
In fear of the torrential rains.
And the languor of the tea and trifle,
Women who sigh like paper cups
Falling to the pantry floor.
The sherbet and the parrots,
Once emblematic of the Asian Kings,
Are no but grim reminders
Of an age composed so much of paltry
things.

Unnamed Poem

I walked into my bedroom (my cat had died
That night), greeted only by the viscous
Smell of burning wax, and a vigil
Of ebbing light, which marched
Across those voiceless tiles,
Pensive, sprawled across the languid floor,
I heard an obscure music
Falling in random order
Like needle shaped crystals of iridescent
light
Forming patterns on a beach of darkness –
Or, perhaps, the rain.
I cried.

Oaxacan Dream

White sails, black stallions, and crates of
stolen spice from Jaffa or Ceylon appear in a
savage climax of colors. Aztec priests with
obsidian knives and frightened daughters
thrown into the red abyss. Oaxaca, light.

Aging Kings in temples of gold and
turquoise surrounded by clay urns striped
with paints made from coffee beans and
crushed berries, thick cones of incense and
intoxicating drinks fill the center of the
room.

Then the flash of sharp helmets and pale
skin. Blood and the thick stench of dead
llamas against the azure sky. Salt-stained
leather and the scream of drowning horses.
Scurvied Africans and soft winds and the
thin ropes of blistered hands. The mirror of
water against a sparkling blade and a
wooden scabbard wrapped in frail cotton
from a woman's dress.

And the dream of Isabella fills the window's
glass. Her soft touch and perfumed hair, her
darkened eyes and her pearl bracelets. And
pewter cups fill her cool tables. Bearded
noblemen deck her veranda with bright
flowers and vases from the furthest quarters

of the Empire. Aqueducts and bridges link
sandy hills where children eat warm fruit
and play with colored birds.

But still the death of Aztec princes in heaps
of wet papaya leaves: burned wrists, broken
sandals and sun-dried wood in the quiet air.